My Reiki Journey

Level I & II

Published by Monica L. Morrissey

Copyright 2023 by Monica L. Morrissey
LLC

https://www.monicalmorrissey.com/

https://www.facebook.com/groups/dimesfromheaven

Instagram @dimefromheaven

made with love

What is Reiki?

"Reiki is a Japanese technique for stress reduction and relaxation that also promotes healing. It was discovered by Mikao Usui in March 1922. Reiki is administered by 'laying on hands' and techniques such as this have been practiced for thousands of years. Reiki is a very simple technique that can be easily learned by anyone."

~ William Lee Rand from
Reiki, The Healing Touch First and Second Degree Manual

Different levels of Reiki

Reiki Level I- opens the energy channels

Reiki Level II- expansion of the energy channels

Master Reiki- Connected to a higher self/intuition

Date:

Why do you want to learn Reiki?

_____

_____

_____

_____

_____

_____

_____

_____

_____

_____

_____

_____

_____

_____

_____

_____

_____

Please refer to www.reiki.org for the following information:

https://www.reiki.org/code-ethics

https://www.reiki.org/standards-practice

Notes from my training

Date:

_____

_____

_____

_____

_____

_____

_____

_____

_____

_____

_____

_____

_____

_____

_____

_____

_____

Notes continued

Date:

Hand positions

Hand positions

Date:

Write about your attunement here:

_____

_____

_____

_____

_____

_____

_____

_____

_____

_____

_____

_____

_____

_____

Using Essential Oils during a Treatment

Before a treatment begins:

- Choose an essential oil
- Rub the oil on the palm of your hand
- Rub your palms together
- Create a tent over your client's nose
- Have the client take a big inhale through his/her/their nose
- Exhale through the mouth
- Repeat this three times

Using Crystals and healing stones to enhance your practice

Black tourmaline- protection

Selenite- cleansing

Clear quartz- healing

Amethyst- calmness

Fluorite- focus

Labradorite- transformation

Lapis Lazuli- wisdom

Celestite- balance

Malachite- prosperity

Aventurine- good luck

Citrine- abundance

Carnelian- Vitality

Rose quartz- self-love

Notes about using Crystals and Healing Stones

during a Reiki Session

- Make sure all stones are cleansed before working with a client.
- Place a stone on the body of the client where you feel energy is needed
- Ask your intuitive self what energy the client needs and refer to the chart on the previous page.
- Cleanse the stones again after the session

21 Reiki Cleanse

Avoid: drugs, alcohol, excessive caffeine, high sugar foods

Daily Suggestions

Reiki meditation

Drink lots of water

Self-care treatment one time per week

Spend time in nature

Journal daily

Dance or exercise

Notes about my cleanse:

Date:

_____

_____

_____

_____

_____

_____

_____

_____

_____

_____

_____

_____

_____

_____

_____

Notes from my training

Date:

_____

_____

_____

_____

_____

_____

_____

_____

_____

_____

_____

_____

_____

_____

_____

_____

Notes continued

Date:

Date:

_____

_____

_____

_____

_____

_____

_____

_____

_____

_____

_____

_____

_____

_____

_____

_____

Reiki Symbols

Note: The Reiki symbols are available to Level II Reiki students. It is important to keep them as sacred symbols so do not share them in this book. This is a space for you to draw the symbols.

Reiki Symbols

Notes continued

Date:

Reiki II Attunement. Write about your   Date:

experience here:

_____

_____

_____

_____

_____

_____

_____

_____

_____

_____

_____

_____

_____

Balancing Chakras using a Pendulum

Training your pendulum

- Hold your pendulum in one hand (I use my dominant hand)
- Think the word "Yes"- and notice what happens to the pendulum. My pendulum spins clockwise but I have seen others go up and down or counter-clockwise
- Think the word "No" and notice what happens. My pendulum either stays still in one place or swings counter-clockwise.

Every one's pendulum is different so just go with what works for you!

Testing Each Chakra for Alignment

Toward the end of a session, take your pendulum and start at the crown chakra and work your way down to the root chakra. If you don't receive a yes, then something is out of balance. Ask what is needed to align the chakra. Sometimes a stone helps or a message to the client. Sometimes the client may need more Reiki energy for a chakra to align.

Balancing Chakras using other techniques

Another way to check for chakra alignment is to use your natural born spiritual gifts. As we have our physical five senses, we have spiritual senses that are similar. They are called our "Claire" abilities. When aligning chakras, some people see colors around the aura of the person. Some may feel an intuitive feeling about the message for the person. Whatever way you tap into your intuition guides you into aligning a client's chakras. Here are the different claire abilities:

Clairvoyance- Clear seeing
Clairaudience- Clear hearing
Clairsentience- Clear feeling
Clairalience- Clear smelling
Clairgustance- Clear tasting

All of these are invisible energy that you have the ability to connect with at anytime. Some claire abilities are stronger than others. Find out which one you are able to tap into to enhance your practice.

Date:

What was it like to give someone Reiki?

How did you connect with your intuition?

_____

_____

_____

_____

_____

_____

_____

_____

_____

_____

_____

_____

_____

_____

_____

Date:

More about the author

Monica L. Morrissey was a public school educator for thirty-two years. Her experience teaching others has helped her gain the knowledge she needed for an unexpected career change: becoming a writer, intuitive health and life coach, Reiki Master and Instructor, Past Life Regression Specialist and intuitive angel card reader. At the age of fifty, Monica shared her inspiring Dimes from Heaven story to help others understand our connection to souls in the Spirit world. Even though her fear of being judged in a world of academia almost crippled her, she stepped out of her comfort zone to help others.

Following her spirit like never before, she began sharing stories about synchronistic events, revealing that our souls never die. As an empath and natural-born teacher, her faith guided her to help people.

Monica has always been a spiritual person but, working in the public school system, she couldn't always share her true self. After the tragic death of her nephew in 2008, she secretly began reading and studying about mediums, death, grief, and how our bodies (and life) are affected by our thoughts. Her retirement from the public school system allows her to follow her true passion: helping people learn more about everlasting life and how to live healthier and happier lives. What if people were able to feel the Spirit of their loved ones after their physical death? What if everyone knew that our souls never die? What if we understood our intuitive abilities that we are born with? What if everyone was in touch with their soul?

Monica's upcoming book in 2023, *Once Upon a Dime Heaven is Talking to Us Do You Know How to Listen?* helps you unlock the invisible key to Heaven so that you are able to receive a sign from your loved one(s).